WHAT ON EARTH IS A
Capybara

EDWARD R. RICCIUTI

 A BLACKBIRCH PRESS BOOK
WOODBRIDGE, CONNECTICUT

Published by Blackbirch Press, Inc.
One Bradley Road, Suite 104
Woodbridge, CT 06525

©1995 Blackbirch Press, Inc.
First Edition

Printed in the United States

10 9 8 7 6 5 4 3 2 1

Photo Credits:
Cover, title page: ©Kevin Schafer and Martha Hill/Peter Arnold, Inc.
Pages 4—5: ©Joe McDonald/Animals Animals; page 6: ©Joe McDonald/Animals Animals; pages 8—9: ©Roland Seitre/Peter Arnold, Inc.; page 10: ©Joe McDonald/Animals Animals; page 11: ©C. C. Lockwood/Animals Animals; page 11 (inset): ©Joe McDonald/Animals Animals; pages 12—13: ©B. G. Murray, Jr./Animals Animals; page 15: ©Luiz Claudio Marigo/Peter Arnold, Inc.; pages 16—17: ©Roland Seitre/Peter Arnold, Inc.; page 18: ©Gerry Ellis; pages 20—21: ©Roland Seitre/Peter Arnold, Inc.; page 22: ©David MacDonald/Animals Animals; page 23: ©David MacDonald/Animals Animals; pages 24—25: ©Henry Ausloos/Animals Animals; page 26: ©John Chellman/Animals Animals; page 27: ©C. Prescott-Allen/Animals Animals; pages 29—30: ©Joe McDonald/Animals Animals.

Map by Blackbirch Graphics, Inc.

Library of Congress Cataloging-in-Publication Data
Ricciuti, Edward R.
What on earth is a capybara? / by Edward R. Ricciuti. — 1st ed.
    p.   cm. — (What on earth series)
    Includes bibliographical references (p.   ) and index.
    ISBN 1-56711-097-5 (lib. bdg.)
    1. Capybaras—Juvenile literature.   [1. Capybaras.   2. Rodents.]
I. Title.   II. Series.
QL737.R662R53   1995
599.32'34—dc20
                                                                94-36827
                                                                     CIP
                                                                      AC

What does it look like?

Where does it live?

What does it eat?

How does it reproduce?

How does it survive?

TURN THESE PAGES AND FIND OUT!

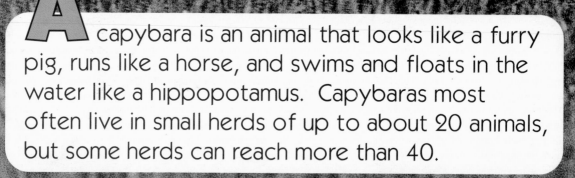

A capybara is an animal that looks like a furry pig, runs like a horse, and swims and floats in the water like a hippopotamus. Capybaras most often live in small herds of up to about 20 animals, but some herds can reach more than 40.

CAPYBARAS ARE FURRY ANIMALS THAT LIVE IN GRASSY AREAS.

OF THE 2,000 DIFFERENT RODENT SPECIES, CAPYBARAS ARE THE WORLD'S LARGEST.

Capybaras are mammals—like whales, cats, cows, and humans. Most mammals are covered with hair, or fur, and give birth to live young. When they are very young, mammals suckle their mother's milk.

Capybaras belong to a group of mammals called rodents. There are almost 2,000 different kinds, or species, of rodents. Gerbils, rats, mice, squirrels, and beavers are just a few of the most common rodents. The capybara is the largest rodent of them all. Big capybaras can grow up to 4 feet (1.2 meters) in length, more than 2 feet (.6 meters) in height, and up to 140 pounds (63.6 kilograms) in weight. Most other rodents are much smaller. The smallest rodent, for example, weighs less than 1 ounce (28.35 grams).

Rodents use upper and lower front teeth, called incisors, to cut and gnaw hard materials, such as nuts and wood. These teeth wear down, but continue to grow throughout a rodent's life.

The name *capybara* comes from a word used by the native people of South America to describe the environment of this animal. The word means "master of the grass." Grasses are an important food for capybaras.

Hydrochoerus hydrochaeris is the name that scientists use for the capybara. This name comes from ancient Greek words that mean "water pig." It is a good way to describe this animal, which has a large, flat snout and lives around water.

A HERD OF CAPYBARAS ROAMS THE GRASSLANDS OF VENEZUELA. GRASS IS A MAJOR FOOD SOURCE FOR CAPYBARAS.

THE CAPYBARA'S PIG-LIKE FEATURES INCLUDE SMALL EYES, SHORT LEGS, AND A BLUNT SNOUT.

Like a pig, a capybara has a thick body, blunt snout, small eyes, and short legs. Its brown coat of fur is long and rough, but so thinly scattered that its skin is visible underneath. Capybaras have small tailbones but no visible tails. Small webs connect a capybara's toes, which number four on each forefoot and three on each hind foot.

The webs help capybaras swim—and they are excellent swimmers. When it is in the water, a capybara can be difficult to see. Only its nostrils, eyes, and ears stay above the surface. Capybaras can also dive and swim completely underwater.

A CAPYBARA USES ITS WEBBED FEET (INSET) TO HELP IT SWIM UNDERWATER.

Capybaras live where the climate is warm. They are found from Panama in Central America through South America to northeastern Argentina. Capybaras live in forests and on grasslands, but usually stay in thickets and other heavy vegetation around ponds, lakes, streams, swamps, and marshes. Some of them live in marshy areas where rivers empty into the sea. When temperatures rise in the middle of the day, capybaras often go into the nearby water to cool off. They also get relief from the heat by lying in the mud. When on land, capybaras will often rest in the shade, sitting upright on their rumps.

TO ESCAPE THEIR HABITAT'S VERY HOT TEMPERATURES, CAPYBARAS WADE IN WATER OR LIE IN THE MUD.

Caribbean Sea

Pacific Ocean

South America

Atlantic Ocean

WHERE CAPYBARAS ARE FOUND

A YOUNG CAPYBARA
PREPARES TO DINE ON
WATER GRASSES. AS
HERBIVORES, CAPYBARAS
ONLY EAT PLANTS.

Capybaras are herbivores, which means they only eat plants. They often stand in the shallows while feeding on water plants. Many water plants eaten by capybaras are soft. The grasses they eat, however, are tough. Chewing off grasses wears down a capybara's incisor teeth, but this is no problem. A rodent's teeth are designed to be worn down before they grow back.

Many different kinds of animals share the capybara's habitat. While grazing in open country, capybaras sometimes feed next to cattle or horses. Other neighbors of the capybara include many types of water birds, huge water snakes called anacondas, marsh deer, giant otters, anteaters, parrots, jaguars, and caimans, which are close relatives of alligators.

CAPYBARAS AND HORSES GRAZE ON
WETLANDS IN VENEZUELA. THE ANACONDA
(INSET) ALSO SHARES THE CAPYBARA'S
SWAMPY HABITAT.

JAGUARS ARE NATURAL ENEMIES OF CAPYBARAS, OFTEN HUNTING THEM FOR FOOD.

Because of their large size, capybaras have few natural enemies. Those enemies they do have, however, are very dangerous predators. Jaguars—the world's third-largest cats—hunt capybaras on land. Caimans stalk capybaras in the water. Giant anacondas also feed on capybaras, although usually only on smaller ones.

When in danger, a capybara's only defense is to flee. Frightened capybaras can run at a full gallop. Often, they try to escape a threat on land

CAPYBARAS WILL FLOAT IN THE WATER TO HIDE FROM THEIR ENEMIES.

by hiding in the water. Hidden by the vegetation, they float among mats of water plants, with only their eyes and nostrils above the surface.

A herd of capybaras is usually made up of animals that are related. Sometimes a herd is just a male, a female, and their young. Larger herds are formed by several related adults and their offspring. Members of a herd communicate with clicking noises, grunts, barks, and whistles. An adult male always leads the herd. He keeps outsiders away, and other male members of the herd in their place, by snapping at them. The full-grown male has a shiny black gland atop his snout

that oozes a white oily fluid. During the mating season, the gland of the lead male grows larger. He rubs the fluid on plants, then spreads it around with his belly. The scent of the fluid is a message to other males that the leader is in charge. This lead male also mates with the largest number of females.

A MALE CAPYBARA RUBS HIS GLAND ON ANOTHER MEMBER OF THE HERD TO SHOW HIS LEADERSHIP.

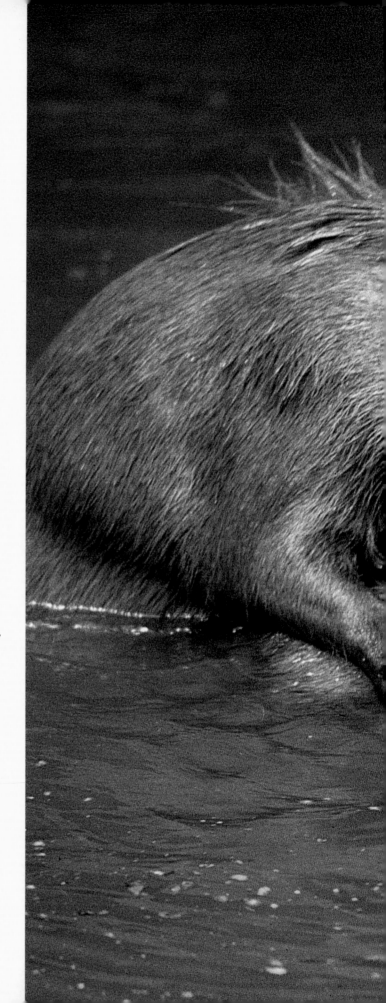

Capybaras can mate at any time of the year. Most of them, however, mate just before the start of the rainy season, which varies from region to region. Mating often takes place in shallow water.

As with other mammals, during mating the male capybara releases sperm into the female. Some of the sperm join with eggs inside the female. This process, called fertilization, results in the growth of embryos. An embryo is a new, developing organism. Capybara embryos will grow and develop within the female for about five months before they are born. Females usually have one litter of young a year. The litter may be as few as two young, or as many as eight.

A MALE AND FEMALE CAPYBARA
IN SHALLOW WATER.

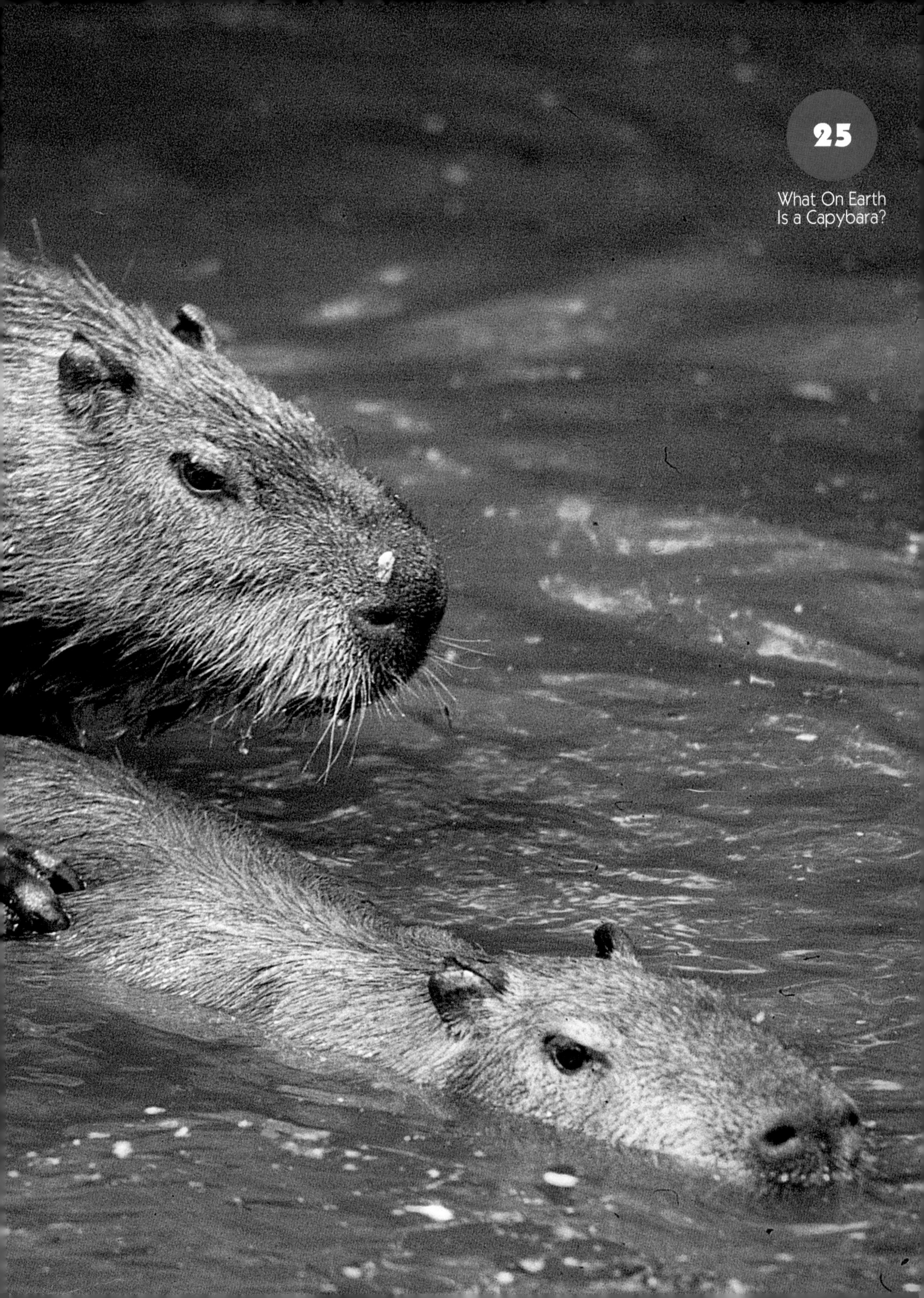

A LITTER OF NEWBORN CAPYBARAS STAYS NEAR ITS MOTHER.

A newborn capybara weighs about 3 pounds (1.4 kilograms) and is a miniature of its parents. Young can stand and run shortly after birth. Although they can eat grass, most young capybaras live on their mother's milk during their first months of life, just like most mammals. Sometimes, several females share the job of suckling the herd's young. At about 15 months of age, a capybara is full-grown and can mate.

A FEMALE CAPYBARA WILL SUCKLE
HER OFFSPRING AS WELL AS
OTHER YOUNG IN THE HERD.

Capybaras are still common in many parts of South America. In some areas, however, they have become scarce, or have even vanished. In many cases, their habitat has been changed by human activities. Draining wetlands to make room for farming and other land development has destroyed the capybara's habitat in many places and threatens it in many other regions.

In some regions, capybaras are also hunted for their meat, hides, and fat—which is used to make grease. In certain places, laws now restrict the number of capybaras that can be hunted. Some ranchers raise capybaras for the market, instead of hunting them in the wild. This also means that instead of draining capybara habitat to create grazing land, the ranchers preserve it, which helps keep nature in balance.

LAND DEVELOPMENT AND OTHER
HUMAN ACTIVITIES HAVE DESTROYED
OR THREATENED THE CAPYBARA'S
HABITAT IN MANY AREAS.

Glossary

egg Female sex cell.

embryo The young organism developing inside the egg.

fertilization The joining of a male sex cell, called a sperm, and a female sex cell, called an egg. Fertilization is a part of reproduction.

habitat The area where a living thing has its home.

herbivore An animal that eats only plants.

herd A group of animals that live together.

incisors Paired upper and lower front teeth.

mammals The group of animals, including humans, that produce their own body heat, have hair, and feed their young on mother's milk.

nostrils Openings in the nose used for breathing.

ooze To be released slowly.

predator An animal that hunts other animals for food.

rodents The group of mammals that includes capybaras, rats, mice, and squirrels.

sperm Male sex cell.

Further Reading

Brooks, F. *Protecting Endangered Species*. Tulsa, OK: EDC Publishing, 1991.

Chinery, Michael. *Grassland Animals*. New York: Random House, 1992.

Cunningham, Antonia. *Rainforest Wildlife*. Tulsa, OK: EDC Publishing, 1993.

Ganeri, Anita. *Small Mammals*. Chicago: Watts, 1993.

Lambert, David. *The Golden Concise Encyclopedia of Mammals*. New York: Western, 1992.

Parsons, Alexandra. *Amazing Mammals*. New York: Random House, 1990.

Sabin, Louis. *Grasslands*. Mahwah, NJ: Troll, 1985.

The Sierra Club Book of Small Mammals. San Francisco: Sierra, 1993.

Taylor, David. *Endangered Grassland Animals*. New York: Crabtree Publishing, 1992.

Tesar, Jenny. *Mammals*. Woodbridge, CT: Blackbirch Press, Inc., 1993.

Tomblin, Gill. *Small and Furry Animals: A Watercolor Sketchbook of Mammals in the Wild*. New York: Putnam Publishing, 1992.

Index